Little
Hawaiian
Cookbook

Little
Hawaiian
Cookbook

Jean Watanabe Hee

MUTUAL PUBLISHING

Library of Congress Cataloging-in-Publication Data

Hee, Jean Watanabe.
    Little Hawaiian cookbook / Jean Watanabe Hee.
        p. cm.
    Summary: "A collection of the best and favorite local recipes from pupu to des
serts"--Provided by publisher.
    ISBN-13: 978-1-56647-793-2 (hardcover : alk. paper)
    ISBN-10: 1-56647-793-X (hardcover : alk. paper)
    1. Hawaiian cookery. I. Title.
    TX724.5.H3H447 2006
    641.59969--dc22

                      2006016945

ISBN-10: 1-56647-793-X
ISBN-13: 978-1-56647-793-2

Photographs on page 5, page 7, page 8, page 40, page 43, page 52, and page 77 © Douglas Peebles
All other photographs by Ray Wong
Design by Emily R. Lee

First Printing, August 2006
Second Printing, July 2009

Mutual Publishing, LLC
1215 Center Street, Suite 210
Honolulu, Hawai'i 96816
Ph: 808-732-1709 / Fax: 808-734-4094
E-mail: info@mutualpublishing.com
www.mutualpublishing.com

Printed in Taiwan

Table of Contents

Main Dishes

Desserts

Glossary

Introduction

Hawai'i, the Pacific gateway to the rest of the world, has become a melting pot of people, so it's no surprise that it's become the same with eating in Hawai'i. Today, a distinctive blend of Asian and European influences comprises Hawai'i's popular favorites beloved among locals and visitors far and wide. In recent years, Hawai'i's diversely mixed resident population has embraced the emergence of new fusion restaurants and the creations of young, experimental new chefs. No matter how fancy a dish is, however, many will never tire of the familiar tastes and flavors of local foods such as mochiko chicken, Kalbi, Spam® Musubi, and Oxtail Soup.

In this collection of more than forty easy-to-prepare dishes, bestselling cookbook author Jean Watanabe Hee has compiled recipes of many local favorites passed on by friends, relatives, and coworkers. A compilation of recipes based on a successful series of cookbooks featuring Hawai'i's best desserts, potluck dishes, pūpū, soups, salads, and sides, this condensed version presents a summary of Hawai'i's most loved and craved foods.

Eating is a treasured pastime of those who live in Hawai'i. Sharing a good meal together is the way we make new friends, celebrate special occasions, enjoy a night out, and take care of our families. Those who are often daunted in the kitchen should fear not as many of these quick and easy recipes can be whipped up in less than 30 minutes, a relief for even the seasoned cook, especially after a long and busy workday. After pouring through and testing hundreds of recipes, what was finally selected are familiar favorites that can often be found at a downtown lunch truck, office potluck, a beach barbecue, and sometimes, even at a trendy eatery serving "gourmet" plate lunches.

Hawai'i is a place where rice is the staple starch, and the mixing of different foods in a meal or sharing various dishes "family style" is a common practice. Whether you choose to eat these entrees with two scoops of rice and one scoop mac salad or not, you can cook for one or for an army all with this one little volume from pūpū to dessert. Enjoy creating a complete meal or a party buffet with your *Little Hawaiian Cookbook*.

PŪPŪ /
APPETIZERS

Curry Mango Cream Cheese Spread

Serves 10–12

2 packages cream cheese (8 ounces each), softened
1-1/2 teaspoons curry powder
1/2 teaspoon dry mustard powder
1/2 cup mango chutney (Major Grey's Chutney brand
   recommended)
1/4 cup sliced toasted almonds
1 box crackers (e.g., Carr's® water crackers, Ritz®)
2 teaspoons green onion, chopped (green part only), optional

Place cream cheese in large bowl to soften; set aside. Mix together curry powder and dry mustard. Mix in mango chutney. Add to softened cream cheese; mix together thoroughly.

In medium-size plastic container with lid, sprinkle almonds and green onions on bottom of container. Spread curry cream cheese mixture over green onions and almonds. Cover with lid and refrigerate for at least one hour. Use butter knife to loosen mold from around the sides of container. Place serving plate on top of container and turn over. Serve with crackers.

Note: This is one of those spreads that is such a great hit at parties that it's passed on from friend to friend. It not only tastes great but also displays nicely. Thank you to Faye Lynn Au for sharing this recipe. This spread is also great with Tandoori Chicken.

Fried Ginger Pork

Makes 6–8 appetizers

2 pounds boneless pork butt, cut into bite-size pieces
    (about 1-inch cubes)
1/4 cup sesame oil
1 cup onion, finely minced
1 large clove garlic, crushed
1/2 cup shoyu
1 tablespoon fresh ginger, chopped
1 teaspoon sugar
2 tablespoons vinegar

Mix together chopped ginger and sugar; set aside. Heat sesame oil and brown pork on all sides on medium-high heat. Add onions and garlic; cook on medium heat until onions are soft. Add shoyu, ginger and sugar mixture and vinegar. Cover and simmer 10 minutes or until done. Serve pork cubes with toothpicks.

Note: This is an old ono pūpū recipe shared by Jean Yoshikane many years ago when we taught at Puohala Elementary School. She says it's also delicious when the pork is cut in thick slices, cooked and placed in Chinese buns.

Spam® Musubi

Makes 8–9 pieces

1 can Spam® (12 ounces), cut into 8–9 slices
8–9 (4 x 7-inch) half sheets nori
2-1/2 cups rice (or 3 rice cooker measuring cups)
Acrylic musubi maker mold

Rinse and cook rice (add 1 teaspoon salt to rice for more flavor, if desired). Fry Spam® slices on both sides. Place mold frame on center of half sheet nori. Place cooked rice loosely halfway into mold. Place a slice of Spam® over rice and press firmly with mold press. Remove mold press and frame. (To remove musubi maker, press down center while pulling sides up.) Fold nori over rice and Spam®. Place musubi, overlapping nori side down on plate. Wrap with waxed paper or plastic wrap.

Variation #1: Teri-Spam® Musubi
2 tablespoons sugar
2 tablespoons soy sauce
1 tablespoon mirin

Heat sugar, soy sauce, and mirin and cook Spam® in sauce before making musubi.

Variation #2: Furikake-Spam® Musubi
Sprinkle furikake over rice in mold before putting in Spam®.

Korean Chicken Wings

Makes 12–15 appetizers

5 pounds chicken wings
2 cups flour and cornstarch combination
2 tablespoons salt
Oil for deep-frying

Sauce
2 tablespoons sugar
1/2 cup soy sauce
3 cloves garlic, finely minced
2 Hawaiian chili peppers, seeded and minced
1/2 cup green onions, thinly chopped

2 tablespoons roasted sesame seeds, optional

Combine sauce ingredients in a small bowl. Set aside.

Mix flour and salt in large plastic bag. Place a batch of chicken wings in flour; shake to coat. Deep-fry. Place on paper towels to drain. Dip wings once in sauce just to coat and place on serving platter. Repeat until all wings are cooked and dipped in sauce.

Temaki Roll

Makes 20–30 pieces

3 packages Temaki Yaki Nori (10 sheets per package)
3 cups rice
1/2 cup rice vinegar
2 tablespoons sugar
1 tablespoon salt

Sesame Sauce
1/2 cup mayonnaise
2 teaspoons honey
2 teaspoons roasted sesame seeds
1/2 teaspoon sesame oil

Filling Suggestions
Imitation crab sticks, cut lengthwise into halves or thirds
Cucumber, seeded and cut into thin strips
Avocado slices, sprinkled with lemon juice
Radish sprouts
3 eggs, beaten and thinly fried, sliced into thin strips
Shrimp, cleaned and cooked
Kamaboko, slivered
'Ahi poke

Rinse and cook rice. Combine rice vinegar, sugar, and salt.
Combine cooked rice with vinegar sauce.

Mix sesame sauce ingredients and set aside.

Select 3 or 4 fillings of your choice. On a large tray, arrange all ingredients, including rice, temaki nori, and sesame sauce. For each serving, spoon a small amount of rice into the center of a piece of nori; top with one or several of the filling ingredients. Add sesame sauce, if desired. Roll into a cone or cylinder.

Oyster Bacon Wrap

Makes 20–24 pieces

2 jars fresh oysters (10 ounces each)
1 tablespoon olive oil
4 cloves garlic, finely chopped
1 bunch fresh spinach, cleaned (or 1 package baby spinach,
     6 ounces)
1/4 cup water
1 package bacon slices (12 ounces), slices cut in half
20–24 toothpicks
1 tablespoon American parsley, chopped for garnish, optional

Put oysters in strainer and rinse with water; drain and set aside. Heat olive oil in pot and add garlic. When garlic is lightly browned, add spinach. Toss lightly and add water. Sauté until spinach is limp and turns a darker green. (Do not boil and overcook.) Drain and set aside to cool.

Lay 1/2 bacon strip on chopping board and add oyster (if too big, cut in half or third) and 1 to 2 teaspoons of spinach. Wrap with strip of bacon and fasten with toothpick. Lay in foil-lined baking pan with toothpick facing up.

Bake at 350°F for 30 to 45 minutes or until bacon browns. Transfer oysters onto serving tray. Sprinkle parsley on top of oysters to garnish, if desired, and serve warm.

Note: Fresh oysters may be found in the refrigerated section at the grocery.

Shrimp Lumpia

Makes 30 pieces

30 shrimp (31–40 count size), about 1 pound, cleaned and
    cut to lay flat
1–2 carrots, cut into 30 carrot sticks about the length of
    the shrimp
1 package string beans (8 ounces), cut into length of shrimp
    (30 pieces)
1 package bean sprouts (10 ounces)
30 square lumpia wrappers, thawed
Oil for deep-frying

Vietnamese Lumpia Sauce
1/2 cup fish sauce (Nguyen Chat Nuoc Mam)
1/2 cup water
1/3 cup plus 1 tablespoon sugar (adjust to taste)
5 cloves garlic, crushed with garlic press
3 tablespoons lemon juice
Hawaiian chili pepper, optional

Carefully separate lumpia wrappers. Lay one shrimp, carrot
stick, and string bean along one end of lumpia wrapper (about
2 inches from edge closest to you). Place a very small handful
of bean sprouts over shrimp and vegetables. Fold end over

shrimp and vegetables and roll once. Fold over sides and roll. Place end down. Repeat until all are done. Fry in 1/2 inch of hot oil on medium heat until brown and crisp. Drain on paper towels. Serve with Vietnamese Lumpia Sauce.

Vietnamese Lumpia Sauce: Combine fish sauce, water, sugar, garlic, and lemon juice. Cut and use 1/4 inch of pointed end of chili pepper to begin with (very hot). Remove seeds, if any. Mix in chili pepper and remove. Adjust to taste.

Note: Sayoko Watanabe created this pūpū when she was running late one day and she had promised to bring lumpia for a party. She improvised and came up with this tasty dish. It was a big hit. Her Vietnamese Lumpia Sauce is also a winner!

Clams and Ground Pork Pūpū

Makes about 8–10 appetizers

1 tray ground pork (about 3/4 pound)
1–2 teaspoons garlic salt
2–3 pounds fresh Manila clams, approximately 1-inch size
1 egg, beaten
1/4 cup green onion, chopped
Worcestershire sauce, to taste (optional)

Place clams in container and cover with water until ready to use. Brown ground pork with garlic salt and ginger. When pork is lightly browned, drain clams and add to pork; cover and steam for about 5 minutes, or until clams open up. Mix in beaten egg and green onions. Sprinkle Worcestershire sauce, if desired.

Note: This is one of David Chun's favorite pūpū, given to him by a good friend. It's easy to prepare and the ground pork mixed in with the clams has a great taste. His wife, Marilyn, also likes it served with rice.

Ono Shrimp Poke

Makes 4–5 appetizers

1 pound shrimp
1/4 teaspoon sesame oil
2 pinches Hawaiian salt
1 tablespoon green onion, finely chopped
Seeds of small Hawaiian chili pepper

Clean and devein shrimp; cut into bite-size pieces. Place shrimp in boiling water for about 5 seconds, or until color changes. Drain and cool. Mix rest of ingredients and lomi into the shrimp. Add chili pepper seeds to taste. Chill.

SOUPS,
SALADS &
SIDES

Easy Egg Flower Drop Soup

Serves 6

Glenn Oura, who lives on Maui, shared
this easy recipe with me.

2 cans chicken broth (14-1/2 ounces each)
1 can cream style corn (14-3/4 ounces)
1 egg, beaten

Heat chicken broth; stir in corn. Bring to boil; stir in beaten
egg.

Hot and Sour Soup

Serves 4

2 cans chicken broth (14-1/2 ounces each) or 4 cups
    chicken broth
1/4 cup lean pork or chicken, cut into strips
2 tablespoons bamboo shoots, julienned
1 tablespoon black fungus, softened in water and julienned
2 tablespoons soy sauce
1/2 teaspoon pepper (or less, adjust to taste)
3 tablespoons cornstarch blended with 3 tablespoons water
2 eggs, lightly beaten
2 tablespoons vinegar
1 teaspoon sesame oil
2 teaspoons green onions, thinly sliced

Heat chicken broth; add pork or chicken, bamboo shoots, and
black fungus. Bring to boil; add soy sauce and pepper. Lower
heat and simmer 2 to 3 minutes. Then while soup is simmering, stir in cornstarch and water mixture, making certain that
it is mixed in evenly. Steadily stir eggs and vinegar into soup
in a steady stream; simmer 1 to 2 minutes. Add sesame oil and
green onions just before serving.

Note: Very quick and simple to prepare and very tasty. Lessen
the amount of pepper, per preference.

Pho

Serves 4

1 package rice sticks (8 ounces)
2 stalks green onions, thinly sliced
6–8 ounces sirloin, partially frozen and thinly sliced

Broth
5 cups beef stock or 3 cans lower sodium beef broth
(14 ounces each)
1 inch fresh ginger
3 star anise
2 stalks green onions, chopped
3 tablespoons fish sauce

Garnish
2 cups mung bean sprouts
12 fresh Thai basil leaves
Mint leaves
1 lime, quartered
Hoisin sauce, to taste (optional)
Hot chili sauce, to taste (optional)
2 jalapeño or Serrano chilies, thinly sliced

Soak rice sticks in warm water for 30 minutes. Prepare broth. Combine beef stock, ginger, star anise, green onions, and fish sauce; gently simmer for 30 minutes. Strain stock; set aside. Prepare garnish on platter; set aside.

Just before serving, bring 4 quarts water to boil. (Also bring broth to boil so broth is boiling about the same time as rice sticks are done.) Drain soaking rice sticks; place in boiling

continued on next page

water and cook for 30 seconds. Drain and divide the noodles among 4 large bowls. Arrange beef slices and green onions on top.

Ladle the boiling broth on top. (The hot broth should be sufficient to cook the meat.) Serve immediately. Let each person add sprouts, mint, basil leaves, etc., from the garnish platter.

Portuguese Bean Soup

Serves 8–10

1–2 pounds ham shank (or ham hock)
3 cans chicken broth (14-1/2 ounces each)
2 cans kidney beans (15 ounces each)
2 cans tomato sauce (8 ounces each)
1 clove garlic, crushed
1 teaspoon pepper
1 medium onion, chopped
4 potatoes, cubed into 1-1/2-inch pieces
4 carrots, cut into 1-1/2-inch pieces
1 Portuguese sausage (10 ounces), cut into 1/2-inch slices
1 bay leaf
1 small head cabbage

In large pot, cover ham shank with chicken broth. Add enough water to cover and boil until tender (about 1 to 2 hours). Skim off fat while cooking. Add rest of ingredients and cook until tender. Continue to skim off fat.

Note: This is my all-time favorite Portuguese Bean Soup. It is so delicious! You can prepare this a day or two ahead before a busy schedule and just heat it up for a quick meal.

Oxtail Soup

Serves 4–6

4 pounds oxtail, cut into pieces
2 cubes beef bouillon (Knorr® brand, Extra Large Cubes)
2 cubes chicken bouillon (Knorr® brand, Extra Large Cubes)
5 whole star anise
4 slivers ginger
1 cup raw peanuts, shelled and skinned
Hawaiian salt to taste
Chinese parsley for garnish

Parboil oxtail 20 to 30 minutes. Rinse and trim fat. Place in pot and cover with water approximately 2 inches above oxtail. Bring to boil and add bouillon cubes, star anise, and ginger. Simmer for 1 hour. Add peanuts. Simmer for another 1 to 1-1/2 hours, or until oxtail is tender. Skim off "scum" from broth. Add Hawaiian salt to taste. Garnish with Chinese parsley.

Variation: Serve with ground ginger and soy sauce as condiments. Serve with cooked vegetables such as mustard cabbage and Chinese cabbage which can be added to soup if desired.

Note: Soak raw shelled peanuts in warm water to easily remove skin.

Imitation Bird Nest Soup

Serves 5–6

1 bundle long rice (2 ounces), soaked in hot water for 1 hour
4 shiitake mushrooms, soaked in water to soften
1 cup bamboo shoots, thinly sliced
3 cans chicken broth (14-1/2 ounces each)
1/2 cup pork, thinly sliced
1/2 cup ham, thinly sliced
2 eggs, beaten
1/2 cup green onions, thinly sliced

Drain long rice and cut into approximately 1/4-inch pieces. Drain mushrooms, discard stems, and slice mushrooms into thin strips. Combine long rice, mushrooms, bamboo shoots, and broth; bring to boil. Add pork and ham; simmer for 15 to 20 minutes. Just before serving, stir in beaten eggs and green onions.

Variation: Substitute green onions with Chinese parsley. Substitute bamboo shoots with 1/2 cup chopped water chestnuts.

Tropics Dressing

Makes approximately 3-1/2 cups

1/2 cup sugar
1/3 cup mayonnaise
1-1/2 cups oil
1 cup catsup
3 tablespoons apple cider
1 tablespoon prepared mustard
2-1/3 teaspoons salt
1 tablespoon Worcestershire sauce
4 teaspoons lemon juice
1 teaspoon soy sauce
1 teaspoon fresh garlic, minced

Combine all in a bowl and mix with beater until smooth.

Note: Highly recommended by Evelyn Shiraki. A fresh great-tasting dressing for your green salads!

Chinese Chicken Salad

Serves 10–12

1 head iceberg lettuce, torn into bite-sized pieces
3 stalks celery, thinly sliced
1/4 cup green onion, chopped
2–3 romaine lettuce leaves, cut into bite-sized pieces (optional)
1 bunch Chinese parsley, chopped (optional)
1 package boiled ham, 8 slices (6 ounces) cut into thin strips
2–3 chicken breasts, cooked in lightly salted water, shredded
20 sheets wun tun pi, cut into thin strips and deep-fried, or
    1 can La Choy® Chow Mein Noodles

Dressing
4 tablespoons sugar
2 teaspoons salt
1 teaspoon pepper
1/2 cup Wesson® oil
6 tablespoons vinegar
1/2 teaspoon sesame oil

Combine dressing ingredients. Place in jar and shake well.

Mix all vegetables and refrigerate. Just before serving, add ham and chicken and toss. Pour desired amount of dressing over and toss. Add desired amount of wun tun pi or noodles; toss lightly.

Note: There are many wonderful Chinese Chicken Salad recipes but this is our favorite. It is simple with a light refreshing dressing. It tastes great at any potluck gathering.

Tofu Salad

Serves 10

1 block firm tofu (20 ounces), cubed
1/2 Maui onion, thinly sliced
1 can salmon (7-1/2 ounces) or 1 can tuna (6 ounces)
1 package bean sprouts (10 ounces), parboiled, drained, and
     cooled (optional)
1 bunch watercress, cut into 1-1/2-inch pieces
1–2 tomatoes, cubed

Dressing
1/4 cup vegetable oil
1 tablespoon sesame oil
1 clove garlic, crushed
1/2 cup soy sauce

Layer the first six ingredients in order listed in large salad
bowl or platter, starting with tofu on the bottom. Place in
refrigerator until ready to serve.

Heat vegetable oil, sesame oil, and garlic until garlic is
browned. Remove from heat and cool. Add soy sauce to cooled
oil. Pour over salad just before serving.

Note: My nephew, Henry Watanabe, often requests Grandma
Watanabe to prepare this salad for him. To me, this dressing is
the best of all the tofu salad dressings out there.

Pineapple Molded Salad

Serves 15–20 as a side dish

1 can crushed pineapple (20 ounces), DO NOT DRAIN
1/2 cup sugar
Juice of 1/2 lemon
2 packages Knox® gelatin dissolved in 1/2 cup water
1 cup small curd cottage cheese
1/2 cup finely shredded mild cheddar cheese
1 cup whipping cream, DO NOT WHIP

Combine crushed pineapple and sugar in saucepan. Heat
until sugar is dissolved. Turn heat off. Add lemon juice and
dissolved gelatin; mix together and place in refrigerator. When
mixture begins to set (about 1 hour), add rest of ingredients
and pour into 1-quart-ring mold greased with mayonnaise.
Refrigerate to set.

Note: When ready to unmold, briefly run hot water over over-
turned ring mold. Place upside down on platter and pineapple
molded salad will drop down.

Hot Garlic Eggplant

Serves 2 as a side dish

1 large round eggplant, cut into 1-inch-long strips and
    placed in water until ready to use (or 2 long eggplants,
    sliced diagonally)
1/2 cup ground pork
1 cup oil

Sauce
3 tablespoons soy sauce
2 teaspoons sugar
2 teaspoons vinegar
2 teaspoons fresh ginger, minced
2 cloves garlic, minced
1/2 Hawaiian chili pepper, crushed (or 1/4 teaspoon crushed
    red pepper)
1 teaspoon cornstarch

Mix together sauce ingredients; set aside.

Heat oil in frying pan until hot. Drain eggplant, pat dry with
paper towels and fry in oil until pulp is tender. Place cooked
eggplant pieces between paper towels and press lightly to
remove excess oil. Add pork to the pan and cook. Remove pork
and pour out oil. Heat sauce in pan until near boiling. Add
eggplant and pork. Mix together until thoroughly heated. Add
a little water if too dry. Serve immediately with hot rice.

Note: This is one of my mother's favorite dishes. She loves
eggplant. The recipe is based on Maple Garden Restaurant's
recipe contributed to one of the Chinese Narcissus Beauty
Pageant promotions many, many years ago.

Hawaiian Namasu

Serves 12 as a side dish

1/2 pound salted salmon
2 pounds cucumbers
Salt for sprinkling
1 Maui onion, thinly sliced
5 stalks green onions, cut into 3/4-inch lengths
2 tomatoes, diced

Sauce
1 teaspoon dried shrimp, chopped
3/4 cup sugar
3/4 cup white vinegar
1 tablespoon sake or mirin
1 tablespoon powdered soup stock (e.g., 1 envelope S&S®
      Original Soup Base)

In large bowl, combine sauce ingredients. Mix and let sit until
sugar is dissolved; stir occasionally. Remove skin and bones
from salmon. Cut salmon in small pieces and soak in sauce.

Cut cucumbers in half the long way. Remove seeds, slice thinly, and sprinkle liberally with salt. Toss to coat and set aside for
15 minutes. Squeeze excess water from cucumbers and add to
salmon. Add rest of vegetables and mix everything together
and refrigerate to chill before serving.

MAIN DISHES

Oven Kālua Pig

Serves 6

4–6-pounds pork butt
2–3 tablespoons Hawaiian salt
2 tablespoons liquid smoke
16 ti leaves (more or less depending on ti leaf size)
String for tying

Cut off ti leaf stems, remove stiff ribs and wash leaves. Arrange leaves in a circular pattern, overlapping leaves.

Score pork butt all over and place in a container. Rub all sides of pork butt with salt and liquid smoke. Place butt, fat side up, on ti leaves. Wrap butt with ti leaves to completely cover and tie securely with string. Place the wrapped butt on heavy aluminum foil and seal well so no steam escapes. Place the prepared butt in a shallow roasting pan and roast in a preheated 450°F oven. After 1 hour, reduce heat to 400°F and cook 3 to 4 hours longer or until done. Shred and add more Hawaiian salt to taste, if desired.

Note: It tastes like the real thing!

Chicken Long Rice

Serves 6–8

2 pounds chicken thighs, skinless and boneless
2 tablespoons oil
1 clove garlic, crushed
1-inch piece fresh ginger, crushed
1 onion, sliced
2 cans chicken broth (14-1/2 ounces each)
2 bundles long rice (2 ounces each), soaked in hot water
Pepper to season
1 stalk green onion, cut into 2-inch lengths

Cut chicken into bite-size pieces (about 1-1/2-inch pieces). Sauté garlic and ginger in oil. Add onion and chicken and fry until slightly browned. Add chicken broth; bring to a boil. Skim off fat and "scum." Lower heat and simmer for 40 minutes.

Cut soaked long rice into 3- to 4-inch lengths. Add long rice, pepper, and green onion to chicken simmering in broth and cook 10 minutes longer.

Note: Rachel Hasegawa's favorite! This is the easiest to prepare.

Lomi Salmon

Serves 8–10

1 pound salted salmon
5 large ripe tomatoes, diced
1 medium onion, finely chopped
3–4 stalks green onion, finely sliced

Soak salmon in cold water for 1 hour, longer if very salty.
Remove skin and bones and shred or cut into small pieces.
Combine all ingredients and "lomi" (massage with fingers).
Chill for 2 hours.

Laulau

Makes 12 laulau

1 pound pork, cut in 1 x 1-inch chunks
1 pound brisket stew meat, cut in 1 x 1-inch chunks
3/4 pound salted butterfish, cut in small pieces
3 pounds taro (lū'au) leaves, washed and stems removed
24 ti leaves, washed and stiff ribs removed
Hawaiian salt to season

Divide pork, meat, and fish into 12 parts. Salt pork and meat to taste. Wrap a piece of pork, meat, and fish in 8 to 10 taro leaves.

Place the wrapped bundle (laulau) in the center of a ti leaf and wrap the ti leaf around the laulau. Use a second ti leaf and wrap around the laulau in the opposite direction, making a flat package. Tie securely with string. Place wrapped laulau in steamer and steam, covered, 4 hours or longer.

Variation: Substitute pork and meat with skinless chicken thighs.

Yaki Tori

Serves 4

2 pounds chicken thighs, boneless and skinless, cut into
    1-1/2-inch squares
1/4 cup sugar, or less (adjust to taste)
5 tablespoons soy sauce
1 tablespoon sherry or sake
1/2 teaspoon salt
1/2 to 1 teaspoon sesame oil
1 clove garlic, crushed

Blend all ingredients (except chicken). Soak chicken in sauce
overnight. Charcoal, panfry, or skewer, if desired, with onion
and green pepper and broil.

Shrimp with Black Bean Sauce

Serves 4

1 pound shrimp, peeled
1 tablespoon oil
1 onion, cut into 1-inch pieces
1 green pepper, seeded and cubed
Salt to season
2 cloves garlic, crushed
Green onion, chopped, or Chinese parsley for garnish (optional)

Sauce
1 clove garlic, minced
1 teaspoon grated fresh ginger
2 tablespoons rinsed and mashed salted black beans
1 tablespoon sherry
1 tablespoon soy sauce
1/2 cup chicken broth
1 teaspoon sugar
2 teaspoons cornstarch with 1 tablespoon water
Dash of sesame oil

In a frying pan or wok, heat oil and stir-fry onion and bell pepper with a sprinkle of salt, until vegetables are crisp-tender. Remove. In the same pan, add a little oil as needed and sauté garlic. Add shrimp; cook until pink. Remove shrimp and discard garlic.

In the same pan, add a little oil as needed and sauté minced garlic, ginger, and black beans. Add sherry, soy sauce, chicken broth, and sugar. Bring to a boil; stir in cornstarch mixture and sesame oil. When sauce thickens, add reserved onion, pepper, and shrimp. Heat through and serve. Garnish with green onion or Chinese parsley.

Chinese Steamed Fish

Serves 3–4

3 pounds whole fish, cleaned with head and tail on
Soy sauce to season
1/2 cup finely chopped green onion
1/4 cup finely chopped fresh ginger
1/4 cup finely chopped chung choi
1 cup peanut oil, heated

Pour small amount of soy sauce in the cavity of the cleaned fish. Steam fish for 20 to 25 minutes in a steamer pan. When fish is steamed, remove and place on a platter. Mix together green onion, ginger, and chung choi, and place over fish. Pour hot sizzling peanut oil over chopped ingredients and fish. Serve immediately.

Variation: If an elongated fish steamer pan is unavailable, chop fish into large pieces to fit in a bowl and place in a round-type steamer.

Note: 'Ōpakapaka (red snapper), kūmū, or other fish that steams well tastes best. A healthy and tasty alternative in preparing fish.

Beef Tomato
Serves 4–6

1 pound beef (sirloin, flank, sirloin tip, round, etc.), thinly
    sliced
1 onion, wedged
2 stalks celery, cut diagonally in thick slices
2 green peppers, wedged
Pinch of salt
1–2 tomatoes, wedged
2 stalks green onion, cut into 1-1/2-inch lengths
Oil for frying

Marinade
1 inch fresh ginger, crushed
1 clove garlic, crushed
1/2 teaspoon sugar
1/2 teaspoon salt
2 tablespoons soy sauce
1 tablespoon sherry
Pinch of pepper
1 tablespoon cornstarch
1 tablespoon oil

Gravy

1 tablespoon cornstarch
1-1/2 teaspoons sugar
1 teaspoon soy sauce
1/2 teaspoon Worcestershire sauce
1 tablespoon catsup (or more to taste)

Soak beef slices in marinade for 15 to 20 minutes. Heat 2 teaspoons oil in pan or wok and stir-fry onion wedges, celery, and bell pepper on medium-high heat for about 2 minutes. Season with salt to taste. Add tomatoes and cook an additional minute. Remove from pan. Heat 2 teaspoons oil in the same pan and sauté beef until medium rare. Remove garlic and ginger. Add the stir-fried vegetables, green onion, and gravy. Bring to a quick boil; turn heat off.

Kalbi

Serves 4–6

4 pounds short ribs, thick cut

Marinade
1/2 cup soy sauce
1/4 cup sugar
1 tablespoon ko choo jung sauce bean paste
4 cloves garlic, diced
1 tablespoon julienne cut ginger
1 teaspoon sesame oil
4 tablespoons finely sliced green onion
1 teaspoon roasted sesame seeds

Slice and "butterfly" meaty part of rib. Score deeply but avoid cutting the bone. Place flat in a container. Mix marinade ingredients and marinate ribs for 1 to 2 hours. Turn every 15 minutes, or use a well-sealed container which can be "flip-flopped." Either broil or grill, turning several times until done.

Note: Always a local favorite at tailgate parties or BBQ gatherings. This original recipe was shared by Carolyn Sur and has been a long-time favorite with her husband Ken's Korean side of the family.

Hawaiian Teriyaki Burger

Serves 6–8

1-1/2 pounds ground beef
1 small onion, chopped
1 egg
1/4 cup soy sauce
1/4 cup sugar
2 cloves garlic, minced
1/2 teaspoon minced fresh ginger
2 stalks green onion, chopped
1 tablespoon sesame oil

Combine all ingredients; mix well. Form into patties. Fry, grill, or broil.

Note: This is definitely a local favorite.

Ma Po Tofu (Pork Tofu)

Serves 2–3

1/4 pound pork hash
2 tablespoons oil
1/8 cup dried shrimps, soaked and drained
1/2 cup chicken broth
1 block firm tofu (20 ounces), cut into 1 x 2-inch cubes
1 stalk green onion, finely cut for garnish
Chinese parsley, cut into 1-inch lengths for garnish

Sauce
2 tablespoons cornstarch
2 tablespoons water
2 tablespoons soy sauce
1 tablespoon oyster sauce
1 teaspoon Hawaiian salt
1 teaspoon chili garlic sauce

Heat oil; sauté pork hash and dried shrimps. Add broth. Bring to a boil; simmer, covered, for 5 minutes. Add tofu and stir lightly until well heated. Add sauce mixture and heat until thickened. Garnish.

Mochiko Chicken

Serves 4

2 pounds chicken thighs, deboned
4 tablespoons mochiko
4 tablespoons cornstarch
4 tablespoons sugar
5 tablespoons soy sauce
2 cloves garlic, minced
1/2 teaspoon salt
2 eggs, beaten
1/4 cup thinly sliced green onion
1 tablespoon sesame seeds (optional)
1/2 teaspoon grated ginger
Oil for frying

Mix everything (except chicken and oil). Marinate chicken for
5 hours or overnight in the refrigerator. Fry chicken in 1-inch
hot oil until golden brown on both sides. Serve hot or cold.
When cold, may be cut into slices.

Note: Definitely a local favorite for parties, picnics, and "tail-
gating."

Lemon Chicken

Serves 4–6

1-1/2 pounds boneless chicken breast, cut into 2 x 1-inch pieces
1 tablespoon sherry
1-1/2 teaspoons soy sauce
1 cup cornstarch
1/2 cup milk
2 cups salad oil

Lemon Sauce
3/4 cup water
1/4 cup vinegar (white distilled)
1/2 cup sugar
2 tablespoons cornstarch
1 tablespoon lemon juice
1/2 teaspoon salt
1/8 teaspoon yellow food color
5 thin lemon slices

Marinate chicken in sherry and soy sauce for 10 minutes.
Dredge in cornstarch, dip in milk; dredge in cornstarch again.
Fry in oil heated to 350°F for about 3 minutes or until golden
brown. Drain on paper towels.

Mix all sauce ingredients (except lemon slices). Cook over
medium-high heat, stirring constantly, until mixture comes to
a boil. Add lemon slices and cook an extra minute. Pour over
chicken; arrange lemon slices attractively.

DESSERTS

Pineapple Upside-Down Cake

Serves 24

1/2 cup butter (1 block)
1 cup brown sugar
1 can crushed pineapple, drained (30 ounces)
1 box yellow cake mix

Preheat oven to 350°F. Melt butter in 9 × 13-inch pan. Sprinkle brown sugar evenly in pan. Drain fruit. Arrange on sugar mixture.

In large bowl, place cake mix with 1-1/3 cups water and 2 eggs. Do not substitute fruit juice for water. Blend until moistened and beat at medium speed for 2 minutes. Pour batter over pineapple in pan and bake immediately for about 50 minutes. Let stand 10 to 15 minutes to set. Invert on rectangular platter.

Haupia

Serves 16–24

1/3 cup cornstarch
1/2 cup sugar
1/8 teaspoon salt
2 cans frozen coconut milk (12 ounces each), thawed

Combine cornstarch, sugar, and salt. Stir in 1/2 cup of the coconut milk; blend to form smooth paste. Heat remaining coconut milk and add cornstarch mixture. Cook, stirring frequently for about 20 minutes or until thickened. Pour into 8 × 8-inch pan. Cool and refrigerate. Cut into 1-1/2-inch squares.

Banana Cream Delight

Serves 24

Crust
2 cups flour
1 cup butter or margarine (2 blocks), chilled
1 cup macadamia nuts, chopped fine

Middle Layer
1 package cream cheese (8 ounces)
1 cup powdered sugar
1/2 container of Cool Whip® (half of 12-ounce tub)
4–5 bananas

Top Layer
2 packages instant vanilla pudding (3 ounces each)
3 cups cold milk
Remaining Cool Whip®

To make the crust: Blend flour and butter with pastry blender. Mix in 3/4 cup of the nuts, reserving 1/4 cup to sprinkle. Press into 9 × 13-inch pan. Bake at 350°F for 25 minutes, or until golden brown. Cool.

To make the middle layer: Beat cream cheese and powdered sugar until blended and smooth. Mix in Cool Whip®. Spread over cooled crust. Slice bananas evenly over cream cheese layer.

To make the top layer: Whip pudding with milk and spread over bananas. Be sure to seal all edges. Spread remaining Cool Whip® on top. Sprinkle with reserved macadamia nuts Refrigerate. Chill several hours to set before serving.

Note: Outstanding! My all-time favorite.

King's Hawaiian® Sweet Bread–Bread Pudding

Serves 24

1 King's Hawaiian® Sweet Bread (16 ounces)
Raisins, cinnamon, nutmeg for sprinkling
3 cups milk
1 cup sugar
1-1/2 cups butter, melted
9 eggs, beaten
1-1/2 teaspoons vanilla

Break bread into large pieces. Place into buttered 9 × 13-inch pan. Sprinkle raisins, cinnamon, and nutmeg over bread pieces. In saucepan, combine milk, sugar, and butter; heat to boiling point. Remove from heat; add beaten eggs. (Be careful that milk mixture is not so hot that it could curdle eggs.) Add vanilla; mix and pour over bread, making sure bread is soaked. Sprinkle more cinnamon and nutmeg over pudding, if desired. Bake at 350°F for 20 to 25 minutes or until knife inserted in middle of pudding comes out clean.

Goodie Goodie Dessert

Serves 16-18

2 cans 7-Up®
4 cans strawberry soda
1 can evaporated milk (12 ounces)
1 can sweetened condensed milk (14 ounces)

Mix all ingredients with whisk and blend well. Pour into deep plastic container with cover. Freeze for 5 hours. Mix again with fork. Refreeze.

Rainbow Finger Jell-O®

Serves 24

4 packages Jell-O® (3 ounces each): 1 each strawberry, lemon,
    lime, orange
6 envelopes Knox® unflavored gelatin
1 cup sweetened condensed milk (Eagle brand)

Milk mixture: Mix 1 cup condensed milk with 1 cup hot water.
Set aside. Mix 2 envelopes Knox® gelatin with 1 cup hot
water; combine with milk mixture and set aside.

Combine strawberry Jell-O®, 1 envelope Knox® gelatin, and
1-1/2 cups hot water. Cool. Pour into 9 × 13-inch pan greased
with mayonnaise. Place in refrigerator to set, about 30 minutes.

Pour about 1 cup of the milk mixture for the next layer.
Refrigerate to set. (Each layer will now set quickly, about 15
minutes each.)

Combine lemon Jell-O®, 1 envelope Knox® gelatin, and 1-1/2
cups hot water. Cool. Pour carefully over milk mixture; place in
refrigerator to set.

Repeat, using lime and ending with orange Jell-O®, with milk
layer between Jell-O® layers.

Hint: Be sure pan used is even, so the layers are even.

Variation: Substitute any flavor Jell-O®.

Hawaiian Chocolate Chip Cookies

Makes 3 dozen large cookies

1 cup shortening
3/4 cup sugar
3/4 cup brown sugar
1 egg
1 teaspoon vanilla
1-1/2 cups flour
1 teaspoon baking powder
1 teaspoon baking soda
1/8 teaspoon salt
2 cups quick oats
1 cup semisweet chocolate chips
1 cup macadamia nuts, chopped
1 cup shredded coconut

Beat shortening and sugars until light and fluffy. Add egg and vanilla; beat well. Sift flour, baking powder, soda, and salt; gradually mix into shortening and sugar mixture. Stir in remaining ingredients. Shape into 1-1/2-inch balls and place on ungreased cookie sheets. Flatten with bottom of glass dipped in flour. Bake at 325°F for 15 minutes or until lightly browned.

Note: It's easy to prepare and has everything to make this a great cookie.

Almond Cookies

Makes 5-1/2 dozen

1 cup plus 3 tablespoons shortening or butter
1 cup sugar
1 egg, beaten
1 teaspoon almond extract
2-1/2 cups flour
1/2 teaspoon salt
1/2 teaspoon baking soda
Red food color
Almonds, blanched (optional)

Beat shortening and sugar; add egg and almond extract. Mix well. Sift flour, salt, and baking soda; add to sugar and egg mixture. Mix well. Shape into walnut-size balls. Place on ungreased cookie sheet. Using thumb, press center of balls to make a depression. Using the end of a chopstick, dip in red food color and place a dot in the center of each cookie. A blanched almond may be pressed into the center if preferred. Bake at 350°F for 15 to 18 minutes.

Note: This is an authentic Chinese almond cookie recipe that was shared by Aunty Clara (Chun). The best almond cookie recipe I have tasted.

Andagi

Makes 5-1/2 dozen

5 cups flour
2 cups sugar
7 teaspoons baking powder
1/4 teaspoon salt
5 eggs, beaten
1/3 cup Wesson® oil
1-1/2 cups water, more or less

Sift together flour, sugar, baking powder, and salt in large bowl. In small bowl, beat 5 eggs and mix together with oil. Pour egg mixture into the dry ingredients. Add water, starting with less and adding enough just until completely moistened. DO NOT OVERMIX. Drop by tablespoon, using a teaspoon to scrape batter off tablespoon, into hot oil (350°F to 365°F) and cook around 3 to 5 minutes, or until nice and brown. Do not crowd the andagi. They will roll around by themselves. Drain on paper towels. Test doneness by inserting a skewer through doughnut.

Hint: The next day, any leftover andagi can be placed in toaster oven at 350°F for about 15 minutes.

Note: This is the well-known Hilo andagi recipe. Easy for beginners and very tasty.

Glossary

A

'Ahi:
The Hawaiian name for both yellowfin and bigeye tuna. Often served as sashimi (Japanese-style raw fish).

Andagi:
Japanese doughnut.

B

Bamboo Shoots:
Cream-colored, cone-shaped young shoots of the bamboo plant sold fresh or canned in Asian grocery stores.

Bean Sprouts:
Fresh or canned sprouted mung beans.

C

Chinese parsley:
Also called cilantro.

Chung choi:
Preserved turnip.

Coconut milk:
The liquid extracted from shredded coconut meat used as milk for cooking.

F

Fish Sauce:
Also called nam pla in Thai cuisine or nuoc mam in Vietnamese cuisine. Very salty and pungent. Made from fermented small fish and shrimp. Available in Asian markets.

G

Ginger:
A brown, fibrous, knobby rhizome that keeps for long periods of time. To use, peel the brown skin and slice, chop, or puree.

H

Haupia:
Hawaiian name given to coconut pudding eaten as is or often used for many coconut-flavored dessert.

Hawaiian chili:
Small, hot, red chili pepper. Substitute Thai chilies or red pepper flakes.

Hawaiian salt:
A coarse sea salt gathered in tidal pools after a storm or high tide. Hawaiians sometimes mix it

with a red clay to make alae salt.
Substitute kosher salt.

Hoisin:
A thick reddish-brown fermented sweet soy bean sauce that is seasoned with garlic and chili peppers.

K

Kālua:
Usually refers to a whole pig cooked in an imu, or underground oven. Substitution: turkey.

Kamaboko:
A Japanese fish cake used mostly in Japanese soup or noodle dishes.

Ko choo jung:
A spicy Korean bean paste sauce used for appetizers or flavorings.

L

Laulau:
Pork, beef, salted fish or taro leaves wrapped in ti leaves and cooked in an imu or steamed.

Lomi salmon:
A fresh-tasting Hawaiian salad of salt-cured salmon, onion, and tomato.

Long rice:
Translucent thread-like noodles made from mung bean flour.

Lūʻau leaves:
The young green tops of the taro root. Substitute fresh spinach.

Lūʻau:
A traditional Hawaiian feast that usually includes foods prepared in an imu, or underground oven.

M

Mango:
Gold and green tropical fruit available in many supermarkets. Available fresh June through September in Hawaiʻi.

Maui onion:
A very sweet, juicy, large round onion similar to the Vidalia or Walla Walla onion. Often available on the West Coast but expensive. Substitute any sweet white onion.

Mirin:
Sweet Japanese rice wine.

Mochiko:
Japanese glutinous rice flour used in making pastries and some sauces.

Musubi:
Japanese name for rice balls.

N

Namasu:
A Japanese vinegared vegetable salad.

Nori:

Sheets of dried and compressed seaweed used in making rolled sushi. Available in Asian markets.

P

Poke:

A traditional Hawaiian dish made of raw fish, Hawaiian salt, seaweed, and chilies.

Portuguese sweet bread:

Bread made with sugar and honey to produce a subtly sweet flavor introduced to Hawai'i by the Portuguese. Typically eaten with meals and not as a dessert.

Pūpū:

Hawaiian word meaning appetizer or snack to enjoy with drinks.

R

Rice sticks:

Also called rice vermicelli, they are usually soaked and served as soft noodles. May be purchased in packages of dry noodles in Asian markets.

Rice vinegar:

A type of vinegar made from rice wine; generally clear with a pale straw color. Generally, rice vinegar has a mellow taste and is lower in acid than other vinegars.

S

Sake:

Clear Japanese rice wine. Other strong clear liquors such as tequila or vodka can be substituted.

Sesame oil:

Oil pressed from the sesame seed is available in two forms. Pressing the raw seed produces oil that is light in color and flavor and can be used for a wide variety of purposes. Oil pressed from toasted seed is dark in color with a much stronger flavor.

Sesame seeds:

Small, flat, oval, white or black seeds used to flavor or garnish main dishes and desserts.

Soy sauce:

A dark salty liquid made from soybeans, flour, salt, and water. Dark soy sauce is stronger than light soy sauce. A staple in most Asian cuisines. Also called shoyu.

T

Taro:

A starchy root of the taro, called kalo, is pounded to make poi. Its flavor is similar to artichokes or chestnuts. The leaves (lū'au) and stems (hāhā) are also used in cooking. Taro contains an irritating substance and must be cooked before any part of the plant can be eaten.

Teriyaki Sauce:
> Japanese sauce or marinade with soy sauce, sugar, and fresh ginger generally used for cooking meats, poultry, and fish.

Ti leaves:
> Leaves of the ti plant used to steam and bake fish and vegetables. Often called "Hawaiian aluminum foil." Substitute banana leaves, grape leaves, or corn husks. Available at wholesale floral shops.

Tofu:
> The Japanese name for soybean curd. Available fresh in Asian markets.

W

Won ton pi:
> Won ton wrappers.

OTHER BOOKS BY
Jean Watanabe Hee:

Hawai'i's Best Quick & Easy Recipes
ISBN-10: 1-56647-901-0
ISBN-13: 978-1-56647-901-1
6 in. x 9 in. • 144 pp
softcover, concealed wire-o • $14.95

Best of the Best Hawai'i Recipes
ISBN-10: 1-56647-842-1
ISBN-13: 978-1-56647-842-7
6 in. x 9 in. • 176 pp
softcover, concealed wire-o • $14.95

Hawai'i's Best Salads, Sides & Soups
ISBN-10: 1-56647-781-6
ISBN-13: 978-1-56647-781-9
6 in. x 9 in. • 160 pp
softcover, concealed wire-o • $14.95

Hawai'i's Best Local Dishes
ISBN-10: 1-56647-570-8
ISBN-13: 978-1-56647-570-9
6 in. x 9 in. • 170 pp
softcover, concealed wire-o • $14.95

Hawai'i's Best Pūpū & Potluck
ISBN-10: 1-56647-518-X
ISBN-13: 978-1-56647-518-1
6 in. x 9 in. • 128 pp
softcover, concealed wire-o • $14.95

Hawai'i's Best Local Desserts
ISBN-10: 1-56647-518-X
ISBN-13: 978-1-56647-518-1
6 in. x 9 in. • 128 pp
softcover, concealed wire-o • $14.95

Hawai'i's Best Mochi Recipes
ISBN-10: 1-56647-336-5
ISBN-13: 978-1-56647-336-1
6 in. x 9 in. • 128 pp
softcover, concealed wire-o • $14.95

Tastes & Flavors of Mochi
ISBN-10: 1-56647-754-9
ISBN-13: 978-1-56647-754-3
4.25 in. x 6 in. • 64 pp • hardcover • $7.95

Order these titles and more at:
www.mutualpublishing.com